MY FATHER'S
TRAPDOORS

POETRY
The Collector and Other Poems
The Nature of Cold Weather and Other Poems
At the White Monument and Other Poems
The Force and Other Poems
Work in Progress
Dr Faust's Sea-Spiral Spirit and Other Poems
Three Pieces for Voices
The Hermaphrodite Album (with Penelope Shuttle)
Sons of My Skin: Selected Poems 1954–74
From Every Chink of the Ark
The Weddings at Nether Powers
The Apple-Broadcast and Other New Poems
The Working of Water
The Man Named East and Other New Poems
The Mudlark Poems & Grand Buveur
The Moon Disposes:Poems 1954–1987
In the Hall of the Saurians
The First Earthquake
Dressed as for a Tarot Pack
Under the Reservoir
The Laborators

FICTION
In the Country of the Skin
The Terrors of Dr Treviles (with Penelope Shuttle)
The Glass Cottage
The God of Glass
The Sleep of the Great Hypnotist
The Beekeepers
The Facilitators, or, Madam Hole-in-the-Day
The One Who Set Out to Study Fear
The Cyclopean Mistress

PLAYBOOKS
Miss Carstairs Dressed for Blooding and Other Plays
In the Country of the Skin

PSYCHOLOGY AND WOMEN'S SPIRITUALITY
The Wise Wound (with Penelope Shuttle)
The Black Goddess and the Sixth Sense

MY FATHER'S TRAPDOORS

Peter Redgrove

CAPE POETRY

First published 1994

1 3 5 7 9 10 8 6 4 2

© Peter Redgrove 1994

Peter Redgrove has asserted his right
under the Copyright, Designs and Patents Act, 1988
to be identified as the author of this work

First published in the United Kingdom in 1994 by
Jonathan Cape
Random House, 20 Vauxhall Bridge Road, London SW1V 2SA

Random House Australia (Pty) Limited
20 Alfred Street, Milsons Point, Sydney,
New South Wales 2061, Australia

Random House New Zealand Limited
18 Poland Road, Glenfield,
Auckland 10, New Zealand

Random House South Africa (Pty) Limited
PO Box 337, Bergvlei, South Africa

Random House UK Limited Reg. No. 954009

A CIP catalogue record for this book
is available from the British Library

ISBN 0 224 03896 6

Typeset in Bembo by
SX Composing Ltd, Rayleigh, Essex
Printed and bound in Great Britain
by Mackays of Chatham PLC

CONTENTS

ACKNOWLEDGEMENTS

Acknowledgements are due to the following: *Baxbr, Chayn-Ys, Grand Street, Haiku Quarterly, London Magazine, Manhattan Review, The Poetry Book Society Anthology 3, The Times Literary Supplement, Verse.*

EIGHT PARENTS

I

At the climax of the illuminated
Book of Hours the Trinity is seen in truth to be
Three self-same white-clad bearded figures
Of Jesus on three identical thrones.
It makes the eyes go funny, like trifocals.

II

This devotional picture resembles
My mother's triptych dressing-table mirror;
When she sat there, three other mothers appeared.

III

The fourth turned round to me and smiled;
The three simultaneously looked back over their shoulders
At somebody out of sight down the glass corridors.
Then she got up, and the thrones were empty.

IV

Nearly a decade after she had emptied her throne, my
    father
Sat himself down in front of the same mirror and died.
He paid his Access- and paper-bill, laid out
Like hands of cards folders on the dining-room table
For his executors, climbed the stairs to his widower
    bedroom,

Sat down at my mother's mirror and saw there were three
    more of him,
Then his heart burst and shot him into mirror-land.

V

Where is that mirror now? you may be reasonably sure
If you buy a second-hand house or bed, then
Somebody has died in it.

V I

But a dressing-table triple mirror? Can you
Enquire of the vendor, expecting nothing but the truth,
'Who died in this mirror?' Death
Leaves no mark on the glass.

THE CHILD

There were stalls in a sidestreet
Blazing with fruit set out to be sold, but I saw
No money pass. The shops got meaner. I stopped
At the Sign of the Iron Spider-Web with soldered in it
Metallic insect fragments – the stark shadow cast
Across the whitewash by the sharp sun deepened
Into a page of scripture. So I went in, through the shop,
And in the back room a woman was giving birth,
The features of the new-born child were just
Clearing the vagina with its eyes and mouth scrunched up
Like a man pushing against a strong wind. Then
Its eyes opened and it smiled and the midwife scooped
It up in her red hands and showed it first
To the mother who laughed and began singing
In a soft voice, and then to the visitor,
Myself; then put it to the woman's breast.

It drank like a thirsty traveller, and, having done,
Raised its sticky head and spoke to me:
'Hello, Peter, child,' it said, and I replied
With my question: 'Are you the elder?' The new-born,
Wet as a fish, replied 'I am'. 'I've brought you nothing
    special,
This was not expected,' I said, 'I've come just as I am;
I've found you, and you can speak.' 'At last,' said the
    baby,
'I can speak; just as you are is fine.'

ARGUS

Argus, in a pulse of waves,
Closing some eyes here, opening
Others there; the long
Light lashes shake out an air
As if his skin were breathing.

Were all the eyes closed
At one time, then he would be
Pelted like a beast with those
Thick womanly lashes, but, no,
The soft-lidded darkness travels
Over his skin in bands;

Were all his eyes wide open
At any one time, then it would be
Like surprising a peacock
Whose whole skin was vivid with eyes;

But they are not, in the iridescent man; those
Which are shut are opening and the open eyes
Are flickering drowsily, and beginning to close
In brindles over the skin, of sleeping, waking:
The opening eyes admire the world outside,
The closing eyes surprise the inner world, and
The opening and closing of the eyes
Winds inner and outer close
And ever more closely together,

Like ropemakers on their long productive walks in sunlight
To and fro between the shadowy boles of avenues.

WEATHER

The glass dropping and rising in the same instant,
Wet air packing round, pressure plummeting,
A skin made strange, as if your veins

Should score your marble limbs in the vacuum
Of the sudden wet heat, then
A deafening noise without any sound;

An exceedingly white cloud
Shadows across a larger whiter one, a blouse
Of water folding white on white leans down

As she quits the shop
Dressed just like that, white on white;
Another soundless clap

That is like a vacuum passing
At which our hairs stand up
Like wheat that knows

It is to be harvested; in the noiselessness
Her heels clatter like nails
Hammered into oak – but then

The glass settles, the barometer
Balances, humidity converses
Agreeably with a few panels

Of sunshine and bows to admit them,
All is propitious of a few hours
Without chills and feverish thunderheat

Glowing back from slates that are
Too heavy for their house, and
The normal echoes of the sea and land

In conversation with the town return.

DA PALACE OF MY FADAH

'Yonda is da palace of my fadah,' the black girl
Pointing to the bull-ring, meaning the bulls.

The man had taken his second bull of the day,
A cathedral of an animal, ears and tail.

He built himself a massive beef sandwich,
He ate it standing up, he washed

The meat and bread down with double X beer.
A warm mist drove up from the sea

And they entered the wetphase for an hour or two.
Then the mist was riven by a wind that smelt

Of hot copper coins, exactly the colour
Of his desire on his breath,

The coilings and shudderings of the tremor
Brought her off the first time,

It was like wrestling with the man
And one other behind him, crescent-crowned;

It was the smell of the bull's blood on his face
Like coins spilt in a furnace did it a second time.

AT THE BUTTERFLY FARM

The hairspring tongue pushed out straight and
Plunged into their favourite dish, their mass,
The mess of punky plums and black bananas,
The rotting syrup which is their feast;

The bushes under the glass roof
In no breeze flutter with the butterflies
Whose gut-vaults are packed with fermenting plum juice,
With the molasses of bananas,
The cellars full of cells in which the soul feasts,

In which the spirit carouses the plum alcohols,
The banana brandies, and translates these joys

Into wobbly flights of magnificent oily garments.

ANCIENT WELL

I

My central heating gurgled like an ancient well.
I thought of God tasting himself in all things.

He was a man bending over a spring
With a wooden ladle in his hand,

Discussing on his palate the taste of the young water,
For only he is truly old;

II

Or he was a man amazed by a dish of mercury
(The trembling mass of electricity which the earth
    contains)

Watching its reflections shiver and settle
To be set shivering again by a Godtouch,

Or, splashed, running in bright orbits
That curve towards larger masses of light

And merge again, without seam, mirroring –
Almost – steady though – divinity catches a glimpse of
    itself

In the molten jewel-heavy looking-glass.

GUARNERIUS

For a moment take into your two hands
The spacious violin, the precious Guarnerius;
Feel a tone in the wood as I speak
Which runs through into your fingertips,
Turning sound into touch, touch into sound;
Put your ear to it, as you would to a seashell;
The tone you feel is an echo of yourself in the instrument.

Like a shell on the shore it is always singing,
The chapelled and multi-mansioned instrument
Plays of its own accord.
Put it on the table; this woman-shape
Needs no maestro,
Sings to bats' cries on the low-voiced wind.

The maestro dilates
Out of its auricles and atria
A cathedral of sound with a thousand altars;
And a million candleflames shattered by applause;
As he bows his head to the audience
The cathedral-ghost vanishes
Into the instrument like a genie into a bottle.

After the applause, laid
Into the shaped velvet of its case,
Open on the bedroom table, it still plays
Notes and tones, like a melodious house
Contracting in the cool night, as his triumph-heat
Fades; he brings his lady back to his bed, it plays
A thermo-acoustic tune which is hers as she enters,
And a sonata as she undresses, and an obligato
As they music each other,

And it plays to them in their dreams
For the dreamstate can hear it;

It will play over and again his death-sigh;

It is a box carved in the shape
Of a windflow angel;

All the maestros who have ever used it
Play somewhere still in this hip-shaped box.

AT RICHMOND PARK

A coppice of strobing pillars and young deer running.

A major deer with twenty tines
And the face of an Original American.

The long grass by the road
Is full of reclining antlers.

The young does as they run
Seem made of glass because their markings
Are like the marks the wind presses
On the flowing grass;

A transparent deer-tapestry with eyes
Blown by the wind over the grass.

SPIDERLY

Specialised hairs in rows on each of eight thighs:
The spiders' ears;

On large spiders, long hairs tuned
To the wingbeats of big insects;

Small spiders have short hairs that listen.
Any sound in the correct range

Will attract a spider, such as a person humming:
Spider-charmer;

Thus to a particular tune the spider eases
Out of his crevice and stands tiptoe

With doubled claws on the piano-polish
Listening with his beards, captured by music;

But beware, there is more: night is a garden
Of winged flowers, and there are nimble spiders

Luring moths because they smell like moths;
Charmer-spider.

SOLID CHAMPAGNE

I

Love on the hills
Among the libraries of rock,
Under the rain their pages darken,
Opening under the rain, closing in the sunshine,
Across some surfaces the rain prints its chapters,
Others deepen into mirrors,
The ultra-violet slate
Slowly eroded by the winds, page off page,
Underpages of new colours, new stone scents,
The whole cliff-walk changing its colours, altering its
    sounds.

II

Many climb into the mountains, into the libraries of ice;
It is so cold here print cannot survive,
All there is is the one white sheet
Screaming with its white noise, its unpublishable affront;
The icy rope which is your path upwards is shagged with
    ice
Like a ladder of knives in the wind's white halls.

III

There was a certain party held on the plateau, on the
    glacier's nudity,
The snow-melt tinkling in the amethyst crevasses
When they drank, and tossed in their glasses;

And after the unpredictable avalanche, the whole feast set
    in the ice
Like a still frozen on a cinema screen,
Floats out later into the slate hinterland,
Into the new-book smell of the water-meadows
In one house-size block on to the rushing brown stream,
The whole original company frozen in a toast,

The champagne solid in the glasses and half-drunk,
The mouths half-open in compliments and breathless,
Not a hair out of place, with frost and brilliantine glossed.

SUCCESS

I

I was invincibly attracted to her;
Only an abyss can exercise such fascination.

II

I paused under a locust-tree, lighting a cigarette:
The water has our mark on it still.

III

She told me at night, the time of living breath;
We took a shower in perfect darkness.

IV

Was that the distant roar of lions
Or the sounds of the clouds travelling?

V

When a pregnant woman bows to a fertile idol
The unborn child bows as she does, within the temple.

VI

So I went out and walked round the lake again
To listen to the sky; approaching thunder
Printed its paw-marks across the water.

FATHERLY

Her father held her attention because
Emanating from his voice and face was
A ghostly genetic prediction of herself;

However long her hair or strange her garments
Her father peered from her face
However she rouged him;

In top hat and tails
Her father put on the glitz
Danced sideways and back again
Tapping his hat-brim
Against his slightly-sweating brow like a rogue;

In pyjamas, her father, tousled and bad-tempered;
In tennis-gear, very much the athlete;
Recumbent in a coffin, her father.

Only in one disguise was her father missing –

She changed herself to a baby –
Her father was nowhere to be seen;

However, when in due time she had a child of her own,
Her father snickered at her from his wicker cradle.

THE YONIVERSITY AT ROCK

(Rock is across the inlet from Padstow
and has remarkable sand-dunes)

I

The unfolding universe she showed me
With her lamps and fire, she
Slender as a lamp-chimney with her arms akimbo,

The fire hanging within, implicit, almond-formed.
Explicit: the lissom glass lamp she carries
With a fish-tail furrowed fire in it –

The shadows unwrap to it,
The explicit light; the implicated
Yoniverse unfolding about it.

II

In the cafe in the sand-dunes
It was all shut surface,
Until it yielded – now

Everything was inset in mirrors,
The polished table-top with its grain
Reflected like a music scoring the tree's years;

A black-white photo of the Eiger
Blew cold wind out of its glass;
My breath deepened in a great sigh

Like an avalanche fallen, a mountainous breath.
Then we walked into the vast dunes' glassware
Which made a musical laboratory to our stride;

It was a one being in its shattered stone;
We clambered through the wind's plait of sands.
I scooped a little in my palm, each stone of it

Shining and discrete: this dust of jewels
Called semi-precious, as if
The sweepings of a home were made of palaces.

III

The abysses of fluid stone rise about us. The wind's rhythms find their explicit statement in the ribbing of the sand. The sand's treasure is implicit, until you take a lens to it. Have you a lens? Or have you only your depression still? There is immense dry wealth on every side. Pebbles have to be polished before they will let the light into their bodies, as the boulders do to a limit: you could employ men to polish the standing stones so that each one became an explicit jewel. But these stones which comprise the sand have at last become small enough for negligent transformation, they have been reduced by endless process until the light can enter them like a queen into her pavilion. Light almost as the light, they have become fluxile, and the dunes are the visual summary of their billions lifted and relaid by the wind into the grasp of the marram grass. Each palmful, lens-inspected, is a spectrum of their colours which in the larger scale and look of distance dissolve to this dune-beige. There plays over these grosser visible registers of small ridge, hollowed dry wave, the implicit spectrum which I have held in the palm of my hand; thus are the levels joined. Clear shards, orange stars, droplets of red iron ore, citrine seeds, greenstones, transparent anvils of quartz and amethyst, granite grains (hovis-coloured) and the sudden amazement of a spiral shell like an empty castle, this pinhead emptied of its cuntish cockle is like a door in the sand, the same cunning shell that on its larger scale weighs your piling papers down. Suddenly the hailstorm lays a jewelled torso across the dunes, and the wind begins a transformation of the scene as if the sand were clouds on the point of gemming into rain.

FISH

Ate mackerel last night;
Dreamed of fish.

Two great fish, taller than men,
Hitched to a fishmonger's ceiling,

The tails still full and stout
Like mermaids' tails,

The scaled carcasses entirely hitched
On two Spanish queries through the upper lips,

The technicolour entrails excavated
Out of the snowy caves of flesh,

But the eyes calm and dark
As though brooding on seas far away and depths
    unplumbed.

As the fishmonger spoke in overalls as white
As fishflesh of fish far bigger than these,

A rich man entered and bought them both,
Had his chauffeur heave them to the car;

One was silver as ocean, the other
Golden as the rich man's abundant hair.

THE FIRE-BOX

Da steht der Tod, ein bläulicher Absud
in einer Tasse ohne Untersatz.
(R.M. Rilke)

He praised his life
Painting with brandy on his breath,
Painting, having drunk enough
To be as flammable as the spirits used
For fiery inspiration, and to thin his oils:
This is the way the spirits join, he said,
Inside a man like me who thirsts for both:
The aqua-vitae and the spirit of death,
Both meet in me and wash over my canvases,

Painting his fiery canvas, cleaning his brushes
In the one you should not drink.

He was married to his model who killed herself.
How could he stop her dying, he protested,
If death were her tipple and she thirsted for turps?
Look! he said, holding up a little turps in a cup
With a chipped lip, that is death!
A little bluish fluid in a teacup.

'Brandy takes its time, is as effective,
I daresay, a slower, better-tasting turps –
It is the fuel, though, which expresses me to my
Festivals of colour, as though
Everything were burning with its own light –
So I pour the great brandies into my engine's furnace!

His paintings chugged with fiery cabs,
The driver and the fireman lit infernally,
Speeding in expresses to the seaside carnival
Where everything blazed with its own self-light.
'She's gone, so I paint what the seaside looked like
When she was with me; that bastard treated her like shit
So she drank turps toasting our life together
Believing I would never take her back, mistakenly.'
I saw the burning carousel, the faces flaming
On the fiery ferris wheel like a round
Christmas-tree. He took a little white
On his brush-tip and changed a screaming face
From woman to man: 'I can't stand
Any face to look like hers in these paintings –
She is the fire, the ferris-wheel, the festival,
I am the express cab brandy-fuelled; have another;
Strange they never give the brandy-brand a woman's name!'

Now he had started on a ghost-house
Full of mirrors or doors shaped like bottles
Into which people peered, and entered, and got lost,
The faces pulled about by bottle-glass, and the images
Mingling, like the merging of two kinds of spirit,
One lively and one dead: 'You could say that my subject
Is really the brandy, not the woman.' I watched him mix
A little cognac in his colours
And drink the rest. He cocked a look at me:
'This libation locked in the paint
Will keep my canvas smelling of my inspiration
Everlastingly; I have done one sketch for her memorial.'

A woman smirking like La Gioconda, one side of her face
Witchy, the other shining with the knowledge of an angel,
A plinth with her dates, a landscape in spring spate
On the left, on the right hand, desert, and on the plinth
A teacup resting, chipped, with a mouthful of bluish fluid.

THE HOT PATIO

The hot patio by the pavilion
Is guarded by two small blood-red stone dogs

On the way to the heavy ponds
Where white swans skin dark tracks

In the emerald scum, and dragonflies
The colour of Martini Rosso, hover

Joined at the tails, exchanging alcohols,
Dart sideways, hang still

In mid-air as though nailed or painted there,
And toads, very cool toads on their stones,

Pant at the throat
And veil their gimlet eyes

With stony skin as they ponder
In their myrtledromes the weight of ponds,

Guarded by the blood-red
Of the two small dragon-dogs.

A PASSING CLOUD

I

They tell of thunder picked up on the teeth,
Or radio decoded on a filling, one's mouth
Buffeted with Sousa; but this was a dull ache
Pouring from a black cloud, I could get
No message from this broadcast, I must have
This radio pulled. 'No,' said my father,
'Keep your tooth, this is but a passing cloud.' I knew
It was him, because that was the brand
Of cigarettes he smoked, 'Passing Cloud' by Wills, and
'Yes,' he said abruptly, 'It's me,' and turned white;
By this token I knew he was dead,
Knew it again.

II

When I had flu I always sweated his smell; his two
    wardrobes
Were exhaling it from hanging woollen shoulders like a
    last breath,
This ancient eighty-four-year-old sandalwood was his
    presence now,
It soaked into me and travelled home and stayed some
    days,
Grief like flu; but I could close my eyes and use it as an
    Inn
To meet up with this wayfarer and imagine him.

III

The cat's way is to spray
And then rub her head in the odour
Like a beautiful woman admiring her mirror-image,

Her portrait thick-painted in impasto pheromones;
This is a cat of magic and she lives
In smell-spirit land as the makers of De Retzke
Printing a black cat on their packets, understand.
That was the other brand he used to smoke
Spraying the tinted air like ostrich feathers,
A chieftain's nose of nostril-plumes,
A rainmaker's cloud he passed, admiring
The sensation in the mirror of the smoke,
The sooth-ing oracle and breaker of time,
The redolent satisfaction that snaps the chain
Into peace and the smell of him
Smoking somewhere quietly in the house.

I V

His presence fills the house when he is smoking,
His nature reaches into every cranny,
Into the carpets and eiderdowns and squads of suits;
The chain is broken now, finis,
And though I can smoke in his house now without consent
The smell of cigarettes does not bring him back,
As he is ashes and has been smoked and stubbed out
'A passing cloud . . .' so that time
For him never forges chains again.

V

Except I notice that being under the weather
I sniff my hand-back and his scent appears; my whole skin
And atmosphere remembers him, the rain falls
And my toothache turns to tears, while the world fills
With reflecting mirror-water fathered out of rain-smells.

FALMOUTH AT FESTIVAL

I

I wake to see
A forest planted in the harbour, all the yachts
Have come in for the Festival;

The harbour is groved thickly,
The water is wood-planked, the woods
Have travelled down the hills on to the waters.

II

The ancient forest crackles with electrical perfume
Crying out: Choose me! Choose me!
Or, choose that one! Our King! It is fitting!
He will make a great stateroom.

III

The trees are walking to the sawmill
In the arms of men, on the wheels of men,
The trunks are secured with the chains of men,
Steel cuts trunk, trunk mills plank,
Plank houses engine; these men
Are carving a yacht from this copse –
It takes years in the seasoning.

Bole upon bole have blossomed sails,
Dazzling shadow-screens, blue, red, white,
They are sailing into their coronation.

V

On the decks under the trees people lay
Their poetry-tables with writing tablets,
Horn mugs and lumps of bread; it is
The National Poetry Convocation, you may sing
Or write your poem and hand it round; the judges
Thread their way across the rhythmic wooden floors.

V I

Simultaneously they hold
The Come Dancing finals
Across the polished decks –
Nobody is confused by this.

EARTHQUAKE ZONE

Our home is an earthquake zone
A town of snapped pillars and hanging avalanches.

To the eye of the visitor all is peaceful:
The small stone cottages, the estuaries
Continually smoothed by the winds, but the reality?

Great rebounding boulders falling from the sky
Several times a day, big as townhalls
Or several streets long.

Where do these falling bodies come from?

I am watching the full moon –
How beautiful and serene as it sails –
Then its black equivalent comes hurtling down
And lands again in some crater made before . . .

But, look! the moon still rides
Tranquil as a postcard;
And yet again its heavy ghost falls.

The moon's concussion echoes from hill to hill.

During fine evenings occasionally
Another apparition visits,

A walled city of towers
And cisterns full of bright water
Alights and fits over our streets,

And we wander through this extra city,
Exploring this astral version of our home town
Which opens galleries out of our ordinary stairs,
Finds a throne-room in every quiet conservatory.

LOOSE FACES

I

A death in the family loosens all the faces.

II

The family face, shattered by death,
Seeks its identity once more
By assembling with all the other family faces.

III

The chief mourners, those closest to the corpse,
Wear their tragedy-masks with the tucked-down mouths.
Many of the faces are set and stern,
Others crumpled like the hankies they periodically
Lift to their eyes; these faces have collapsed
Into their structure and wear a glass mask of tears.

IV

The pews are like a family tree of faces
Ripening for their turn among the bereaved or in the box.

V

The funeral does not straightaway glue
The loosened faces back on again, this will take
A couple of years and even then
You may not get the same face back
As you entered the funeral with. Possibly due
To your visualisations of and prayers for the departed one
His or her face may drop like a tribal mask over your own
Grappling into the bony slots and runners provided,
And this is the face of the next one in the firing-line.

VI

There are several alternative family faces at the funeral,
  these
Joined themselves together at their weddings, the
  alternative festival
Where facial melodies are fused creating entirely new
  themes.

VII

For many weeks after the funeral he was without wishing
  it
All the dead people who had composed him without his
  permission;
He thought he had no affinity at all with his father's
  mother
But there she was in his place reflected in a shop window
Dressed in a man's jersey and without her jabot of lace;
A reality photograph of his father, bulky and upright
And wearing dark glasses made to his prescription
Came and sat down in his body; that was more than a
  face,
That was the whole being of the dead person in a stolid
  mood.

VIII

These faces flew about the crematorium chapel like putti
And alighted where they would; the people made fluid
By their flux of grief only had to gaze into the eyes
Of one closely-related and charged with weeping
To turn into that person, even setting into a deathmask.

WAXHOUSE

The waxworks are stock-still.
The music played to accompany them has stopped

Going up and down the tubes of the automaton
Pipe–organ, the only moving figure having been

A small Mozart clashing a cymbal.
Like all waxworks they have always just stopped moving.

The Commissar is astride his blackwax stallion;
The General sits in his wax on his great grey wax horse;

They wear the original uniforms and leather reins,
And saddles, and gold braid

On their shoulders as if the sun had shat on them.
Why is the wax unutterably so still? because

This stopped music has stopped them stiller than before,
Overstill, down to the splashes of wax blood

Gouted to the General's flourished sword.
(Know that when the music of the heart stops

And the body cools in death, the liquid oil,
The brilliantine in which all the tissues are bathed,

Curdles to hard and solid fat, like a waxwork.)

POEMS OF PARASYN

I

After the storm, the air is full
Of fierce rainbows. A slow blue flash
Suddenly across the Fal – a mist
Illuminated by a patch of blue sky
Clearing off-scene – floating neon,
Bluebell-semen.

II

Alder – glutinous and bloody.
From it you get three fine dyes:
Red from the bark, green from the flowers,
Brown from the twigs. The wood when felled
Is at first white, then it bleeds crimson,
Like a man. The colours to some
Signify water and earth,
And in the wood the red power of fire
To rid the earth of cold-creating water.

III

There is a pack of small birds
Feasting on the fallen apples which
Lie thick as cobbles under the trees.
A cat jumps in from the low wall
And they fly up in one wheeling wing,
Hook on the taut telephone wires and sit
In still rows, crapping. The cat remains
Among the wasps which do not hurt the birds

But which worry the cat who swats at them
And in due time retreats. Then the birds return
And feast in company with the wasps again
Who mine deep and invisible their galleries of fruit.

IV

A little beetle like an ornamental box
Studded and hasped and protecting what elixirs!

V

When she woke me I was dreaming and it seemed
My body was covered with winged interlacing figures,
The skin a living tapestry depicting other regions.
A special chemism would be discovered, and a sanctuary
That is a copy and shadow of what is in heaven,
Called Parasyn.
I dressed in clothes loose as a tree's clothes; it was
Because I had given up my job, and everything
Looked glittering and shining. There was also
A book of masochism
That contained diagrams explaining the universe.

VI

I watched a cleft in the road which in particular shone –
It was full of beautiful spiders – including one grey
Long-bodied one who lingered in a perfect symmetry
Of its legs, its web.

CHEMISTRY

I

Weather opens the doors in the head and claps them to,
Opens them gently in a gradual suffusion of sun,

Then thunder-coloured gates slam shut; after, there is that
    peace
As the sky swings wide all its doors, which disappear

As they open. He walks out into his garden, what is this
Gelatinous alga that wobbles on his lawn after

Continuous rain? It must be that fat of manna, called
Maydew, a star-jelly or witch's butter, a ray

Or radiation of a certain star, or its off-scouring
Cast to earth. But what is it actually? He tastes it,

The oil spreads through the porches of his brain
Which is now a nest of rainbows. It is exterior soul.

II

His soul, that rainbow-spot in the brain,
Which resembles the rainbow of a chrism oil

Spreading over the grey hulls inside his skull, expands
Like an Adam's tree of paradise with many flowers,

This oil film sensitive to all forces, weaving
This way that, as the wind scuds. The balsam

Of this edible rainbow sweats from the heart and is
    exhaled
On the breath; like oil that spreads across a marsh,

An impalpable, tremulous organ, this rainbow.

III

I light a match, and the exaltations
Of the darkened nettles in the darkening garden

Burn too, and let the colour of the small flame into
Their poisonous chambers, and as I move about the
    garden,

The small flame in my hand, how many
Toxic dews reflect me!

Pierced on their sparking thorns,
Preparing assassination as my image floats

In the ozonous nettle-bank with its matchlight.

VAUX HILL

Vaux Hill is now Moon-on-the-Water Hall
Where Ms Satinhammer sits
Observing the night moths and beetles
Flying their chandelier patterns
Of horn and juice
Which light with insect light
The shelving winds of Vaux Hill.

Many people have gathered
In the darkness to fly kites
Like big paper ghosts
Or gigantic evening moths
Hissing above them on the slopes.

Satinhammer suddenly knew
She was Our Lady of the Dark Woods
In the moment that the dark
Came in with one stride.

All we see of the trees now
Is their perfume;
It is the same as hers;
We feel the touch of night moths
Which is her touch.

CLIMAX FOREST

A neat sunlit room
Filled with country arts –
Needlework and quilts.

A backwoods school of architecture:
Frame, a wide porch,
Deep eaves, a heavy

Gently-pitched roof –
Perhaps the house
Of a sawmill operator

Predatory of the huge
Climax forest that once
Blanketed nearly all

Of North America, but
He living within its construct,
Flesh of its flesh.

It had been a beautiful
Day, and the beauty deepened.
In the orange light

The long grasses at the edge
Of the garden seemed spun
From gold. The two

Had promised not to speak. She
Got into bed and like a vast
Nesting bird settled on him. It became

Like watching the river
For hours, watching
All the places it had wetted.

MORIA

During the day he served her
Black meals: milkless coffee,
Tenebrous grain bread spread with molasses,
Passion-fruit dessert with pomegranates
On black glass plates on a golden tablecloth,
And what garments they pleased.

At night it was a white meal,
Boiled fish and spumanti
Lost almost on snowy napery;
He dressed in black, and laid out for her
Bridal white each night.

One day she understood
This conduct was a joke
Against himself, and not her.

So that day when he returned
She had spread the table
With a cloth of threads of very many colours,
And she served him a portion of saffron rice
And scarlet curry off nursery plates
Illustrated with rainbows and teddy-bears,
And they finished with little lung-pink cakes
Dressed with hundreds and thousands
And they sat down by the bright flames
Where she offered him in a bowl
Ballarat apples (Green with a red blush)
Sturmer Pippins (Green blushing bronze) and
Wax-clean Golden Delicious, but he refused
And chose to drink them in their spiritual form
As sprightly Calvados.

BLACK BONES

That is a human skeleton under the cataract,
The jet bones shining in the white noise,
The black bones of a man of light;

It is a cascade that accepts
Human form from the bones
That have walked into it, and stand;

It must have been his method of death
To walk into a waterfall and be washed away,
Licked clean down to the jetting bones;

And the bones articulate the roar
Of the cataract that seems to speak
Out of the ribs and skull:

His white-haired sermon from the pelting brow,
The unfathomable water-lidded sockets;
Clad in robes that are foam-opulent,

And never the same clothes twice.

STAINES WATERWORKS

I

So it leaps from your taps like a fish
In its sixth and last purification
It is given a coiling motion
By the final rainbow-painted engines, which thunder;
The water is pumped free through these steel shells
Which are conched like the sea –
This is its release from the long train of events
Called *The Waterworks at Staines*.

II

Riverwater gross as gravy is filtered from
Its coarse detritus at the intake and piped
To the sedimentation plant like an Egyptian nightmare,
For it is a hall of twenty pyramids upside-down
Balanced on their points each holding two hundred and fifty
Thousand gallons making thus the alchemical sign
For water and the female triangle.

III

This reverberates like all the halls
With its engines like some moon rolling
And thundering underneath its floors, for in
This windowless hall of tides we do not see the moon.
Here the last solids fall into that sharp tip
For these twenty pyramids are decanters
And there are strong lights at their points
And when sufficient shadow has gathered the automata

Buttle their muddy jets like a river-milk
Out of the many teats of the water-sign.

I V

In the fourth stage this more spiritual water
Is forced through anthracite beds and treated with poison
    gas,
The verdant chlorine which does not kill it.

v

The habitation of water is a castle, it has turrets
And doors high enough for a mounted knight in armour
To rein in, flourishing his banner, sweating his water,
To gallop along this production line of process where
There are dials to be read as though the castle library-
Books were open on reading-stands at many pages –
But these are automata and the almost-empty halls echo
Emptiness as though you walked the water-conch;
There are very few people in attendance,
All are men and seem very austere
And resemble walking crests of water in their white coats,
Hair white and long in honourable service.

V I

Their cool halls are painted blue and green
Which is the colour of the river in former times,
Purer times, in its flowing rooms.

42

VII

The final test is a tank of rainbow trout,
The whole station depends on it;
If the fish live, the water is good water.

VIII

In its sixth and last purification
It is given a coiling motion
By vivid yellow and conch-shaped red engines,
This gallery like the broad inside of rainbows
Which rejoice in low thunder over the purification of
    water,

Trumpeting Staines water triumphantly from spinning
    conches to all taps.

SNOW BONFIRE

Car headlights snap and flash
In the snowbank, immense hall
Of tiny mirrors blue as electricity.

We had lighted a bonfire
And it emitted its pharmacopeias –
Then there was a sudden snow-squall
And flakes snapped like buds of ointment,
They fizzled and vanished on the hot logs.

The snow looked like a pharmacist
In a white coat moving about his magisteries,
His dangerous medicines;
He was perfumed so strongly you could hardly see him;
Part of him was made of smoke and part of snowflurry.

The trees in the fire
Were turning to light
And perfumery forests
Where the white-coated one ran,
Gathering, a white shadow.

It was a struggle of powers
As when the thunderstorm drenches the lava-fields,
Their red pulses to black in the cold torrents
Until there evolves a dragging river of mist.

II

He throws hot stones into the snowbank.
They rush and hiss like underground trains.

They do not brake until they are cold.
I have made in this mane of white
Eyes, ears and a mouth without meaning to.

STORYDAD

I

We did not know we were on the ships
That throbbed grandly between the endless
Horned islands until the professional

Story-teller told us just that, and we saw them
All around, jungle-islands sliding past the ports,
The triple pulse of the ship, the foam-crescent islands;

We were in fact at home and he was our picture-daddy.
He was the place that was always healing
In happy endings, breaking out and healing.
He was a hobbling cottager, his roof leaked
In the great rains during story-telling, and he recruited
The water-voices to reconstruct the South Seas,
But the dampness hobbled him – why should he care
When he had these stories for speaking furniture?

II

I came in while he was talking
To no one, for he was blind, and had no idea
Once the stories started if there were listeners near.
Upright in his rush-bottomed chair,
The tales continued day and night, with a short repose,
And when asleep he dreamed in silence until one
Came up to him and laid fingers on his eyes
Which during dream-time throbbed
Grandly; and the tale proceeded.

Then once I touched his penis and he fell
Silent. I gripped it in my hand
And it seemed as though he were reading
Though silent, many tales aloud to me through it.
Eventually he will retire to Iron Mountain, to a hermitage
Of slate, haematite and vine. I will visit
My picture-daddy there, and he
Will tell me until he dies stories through his penis,
And after that, resounding through the whole iron
    mountain.

MY FATHER'S TRAPDOORS

I

Father led me behind some mail-bags
On Paddington Station, my grief was intense,
I was a vase of flowing tears with mirror-walls,

He wore a hard white collar and a tight school tie
And a bristly moustache which is now ashes
And he took me behind the newsprint to kiss me hard,

The travelling schoolboy,
And his kiss was hungry and a total surprise.
Was it the son? Was it the uniform?

It was not the person, who did not belong
Not to father, no.

II

He drove a hole-in-one. It flew
Magnetised into its socket. He'd rummy out
While all the rest shuffled clubs from hearts.
He won always a certain sum on holiday

At any casino; called it his 'commission'.
He could palm cards like a professional.
He had a sideboard of cups for everything

From golf and tennis to public speaking.
He took me to magic shows where people
Disappeared and reappeared through star-studded

Cabinets with dark doors, and magicians
Chased each other through disappearance after
    disappearance.
He sat down in front of my dead mother's mirror

And disappeared himself, leaving
Only material for a funeral.

III

I looked behind the dressing-table
Among the clooties of fluff and the dust,
I looked under the bed and in the wardrobe

Where the suits hung like emptied mourners,
I looked through the shoes and the ironed handkerchiefs
And through a cardboard box full of obsolete sixpences,

I looked in the bathroom and opened the mirror,
Behind it was aspirin and dental fixative,
I looked through the drinks cabinet full of spirits,

And I found on the top of the chest-of-drawers
Where there was a photograph of my dead mother,
My living self and my accident-killed brother,

A neat plump wallet and a corroded bracelet watch
And a plate with one tooth which was hardly dry,
And I looked down the toilet and I turned

All the lights on and I turned them off,
But nowhere in the bedroom where he sat down
And fell sideways in a mysterious manner

Could I find how he did it, the conjurer
Had disappeared the trapdoor.

IV

It was easy to disappear me.
He was doing it all the time.
I did not return that bristly kiss.

On my fourth Christmas there were so many toys
I disappeared into them thoroughly,
There was a silver crane on my mother's counterpane

It was faulty but I did not want it returned,
I have reappeared and so has it,
Nearby and grown-up in the Falmouth Docks,

And there was a conjurer's set
With ping-pong balls that shucked their shells
From red to amber, amber to green,

With a black-white wand that would float,
And half-cards and split rings as tawdry
As going up on the stage among the trapdoors

And meeting Maskelyne close-up, his cuffs were soiled –
White tie and tails should be spanking clean,
My father's would have been, and I hoped

The conjurer would not kiss me,
It would disappear me.

V

He could wave his wand casually
And I would reappear elsewhere;
Once in bed at ten cuddly with mother

He waved a wand in his voice
And I got out of the silken double-cabinet
For ever.

VI

The rough kisses come round the door.
I give rough kisses myself, I am as bristly.
I am not a woman or a little boy.

And I can frighten her or make her disappear
Temporarily so she has to go to find herself
Again in the mirror somewhere;

But having learned this I am careful not to do it.
I do it less than I did.
I did not ask for this bearded equipage.

VII

It has taken me a long while
To appreciate this wedding-tackle at its worth.
My father gave it to me like a conjuring-set.

I do not use my wand to disappear you,
I am rather too fond of disappearing it myself,
But I also use it to empower us both,

It is the key to a wonderment openness
Like turning inside-out harmlessly
Among lights, turning

Over in bed into someone else.

VIII

The conjurer in his soup-and-fish
Vanishes into his cabinets,
His rival reappears, they cannot bear

To be together on the stage
Not while they're dressed in their power
Of black whiteness with starched bows

And cuffs that make the hands flash
While explaining here's a new trick:
The Chinese Cabinet.

It is a silk tent with a front door
As black and tall as Downing Street.
This must be a special trick, shall I expect

Mr Major to ride out on a white horse?
Three people with slant eyeliner have erected it,
They are dressed as spirits who seem

Of the one sex which is both sexes,
And this cabinet is not coffin-like,
No, not at all, what coffin

Would be painted with sun, moon and stars?
A Grand Mandarin with a little drum comes in,
And throws an explosive down as conjurers will

So that the tent shivers and collapses –
Yes, it is a wardrobe that has disappeared all the clothes,
The white tie and tails, the sponge-bag trousers, the
    soup-and-fish,

For someone is coming through stark naked
And it feels good to him
For he is laughing and the mandarin bows as if proud of
    him,

He who touches everywhere for all clothes are gone,
Why, he's in the buff and happy as Jesus save that
His lean rod is floating out just as it should,

Floating like my own, pleased to be like him.